THE MEASURE OF CHRIST

His All-Inclusiveness and His Universality

Dr. Ronald E. Cottle

The Measure of Christ

© 2022 by Dr. Ronald E. Cottle All rights reserved.

This book is protected under the copyright laws of the United States of America. This book may not be copied or reprinted for commercial gain or profit. The use of short quotations or occasional page copying for personal, or group study is permitted and encouraged. Permission will be granted upon request. Unless otherwise indicated, Scripture quotations are from the King James Version of the Bible.

REC Ministries
664 Sweetwater Drive
Cataula, GA 31804
www.roncottle.com

Unless otherwise noted, Scripture is taken from the New King James Version of the Bible, World Bible Publishers, Inc., Iowa City, IA. Other translations quoted:

NIV — New International Version, Copyright © 1973, 1978, 1984 by International Bible Society, Zondervan Publishing House. Used by Permission

NKJV — New King James Version, Copyright © 1982, Thomas Nelson, Inc. Used by Permission

AMP — Scripture quotations taken from the AMPLIFIED BIBLE, Copyright © 1954, 1958, 1962, 1964, 1965, 1987 by The Lockman Foundation. Used by permission. (www.Lockman.org)

NLT — HOLY BIBLE, NEW LIVING TRANSLATION, Copyright © 1996 by Tyndale Charitable Trust.

TABLE OF CONTENTS

PART ONE:
HIS ALL-INCLUSIVENESS

CHAPTER 1: TEXTS & INTRODUCTION

Texts

19 My little children, for whom I labor in birth again until Christ is formed in you. (Galatians 4:19)

7 But to each one of us grace was given according to the measure of Christ's gift. (Ephesians 4:7)

27 To them God willed to make known what are the riches of the glory of this mystery among the Gentiles: which is Christ in you, the hope of glory. (Colossians 1:27)

5 Examine yourselves as to whether you are in the faith. Test yourselves. Do you not know yourselves, that Jesus Christ is in you? — unless indeed you are disqualified. (2 Corinthians 13:5)

29 For whom He foreknew, He also predestined to be conformed to the image of His Son, that He might be the firstborn among many brethren. (Romans 8:29)

13 Till we all come to the unity of the faith and of the knowledge of the Son of God, to a perfect man, to the measure of the stature of the fullness of Christ. (Ephesians 4:13)

Introduction

These verses have one thing in common focus. Though the doctrines are powerful, and the truth is great, it is not doctrine or truth that are in common in these texts. Though the knowledge revealed in these texts is deep, it is not the deep knowledge that binds these texts together, nor is it the ministry described. It is simply the Lord Who is the measure of all things. He is the common Focus.

This book is a meditation on the full measure of Christ. It is intended to help us to dwell upon God in Christ as the measure of our faith and the standard of our discipleship. What is meant by "the full measure of Christ" will be fleshed out and applied.

CHAPTER 2: THE OBJECT OF THE FATHER

The object of the Father from first to last is the Son. The Lord Jesus Christ shall fill all things, and all things shall be filled with Christ. Put another way, this says: "The value of everything in the eyes of God is determined by the measure of Christ in it" (TAS). It is from that standpoint alone that God gauges the importance of everything. How much of Christ is in it? That sets its value with God!

This is of crucial importance today in a world where methods and techniques tend to replace presence and dependence on God. The Church is comfortable with sure business practices for attracting and serving consumers. Church websites are almost exclusively designed for the purposes of competition between churches for the existing

Christians who are in the community as they shop and compare churches for the best fit for them, for their needs.

Leadership practices with which most of today's churches are built are the very same that Christ warned His disciples against, "Their great ones exercise authority over them. Yet it shall not be so among you" (Mark 10:42b-43a). How difficult it is to resist taking control of the Church from the Holy Spirit's leadership. How difficult it is for the members of the Church to resist a "strong" leader, a "great one." But we must learn this. We cannot measure the kingdom of God by human metrics, by numbers, by financial success. We can only measure by the measure of Christ.

But if this is our ruler, our measuring stick, it will make a huge difference; much will have to be cut away because it does not manifest the Lord Jesus. God has set Jesus as Lord of all, and His eyes are looking for Him only in all we do and speak. In God's eyes, the real value of everything is determined by THE MEASURE in which it manifests and glorifies His Son! We must be very careful, and brutally honest as we evaluate our activity and mission, our fellowship on the measure of Christ.

CHAPTER 3: THE ALL-INCLUSIVENESS OF CHRIST

Christ is all-inclusive. Anointed ministry, spiritual revelation, divine calling, even ultimate glorification have no existence apart from Christ. They are not "things" as things in themselves. They are worthless, even diversionary if they are not deeply embedded in the person of Jesus!

Consider John 15:4-6:

> 4 Abide in Me, and I in you. As the branch cannot bear fruit of itself, unless it abides in the vine, neither can you, unless you abide in Me.

> 5 I am the vine, you are the branches. He who abides in Me, and I in him, bears much fruit;

for without Me you can do nothing. 6 If anyone does not abide in Me, he is cast out as a branch and is withered; and they gather them and throw them into the fire, and they are burned.

Why must we abide in Him alone? Because it is Christ alone Who can bear fruit. Any "good" thing we do apart from Christ will be empty, devoid of power, devoid of the will of God. Empty things and dead works are part of what is cast "into the fire" as worthless.

To many Christians, salvation is a "thing," a "possession." It is detached, a gift I receive by itself. It is for my good and makes me different. NO! It is Christ Himself Who is my salvation! He is within me as my salvation. He is not just my Savior (the One Who gives me salvation), *He IS the salvation itself in me.*

Others see sanctification (spiritual maturity) as a "thing," a place I have attained, an accomplishment achieved. NO! "He is made unto me wisdom, righteousness, sanctification, redemption!" (see 1 Corinthians 1:30). He – Jesus in me – is all these! He is not the Bringer of the gifts; He is the One gift of God Who is all of these in all of us.

Colossians 3:3 says, "For you died, and your life is hidden with Christ in God." Then in verse 11 it says, "there is neither Greek nor Jew, circumcised nor uncircumcised, barbarian, Scythian, slave nor free, but Christ is all and in all." And further down in the same chapter in verse 17 it says, "And whatever you do in word or deed, do all in the name of the Lord Jesus, giving thanks to God the Father through Him."

We have died with Christ in our rebirth and baptism with Him. We have been raised with Him. We can do nothing apart from Him. He is all-inclusive in salvation, sanctification, and mission.

CHAPTER 4: "OUR" MINISTRY, ANOINTING, CALLING

It is the same with "our" ministry, "our" anointing, "our" calling. None of these is "ours;" none of these is "a thing" apart from Jesus. Jesus is not only my salvation and spiritual growth. Jesus is also my calling, my anointing, and my ministry.

I have often been told that "I am saved to minister (serve)." This is a dangerous slogan. This mindset makes it easy to see my motive as the ministry itself and not the Lord. We may be so driven by the ministry that we forget the Lord. We have detached the "thing" from the Person, and we are gripped and enmeshed in the demands of ministry in-itself of ourselves.

This always leads to "burn out" and ends in tragedy. When the ministry becomes impossible and unbearable, we "resign" and "quit." This proves that we have separated the work from the Lord Himself.

One more word at this point... What about glorification? We sing hymns about that. We push it out to some future day, in "heaven," above and beyond the here and now. What is important to understand about glorification is that God means it to begin here and start its manifestation now, in this life. What is glorification? It is the full manifestation of Jesus Christ in us!

All of these "things" are not things apart from Him. Salvation is not "something." It is the mighty incoming of a Person. Sanctification is not "something." It is a fuller maturing in the Person of Christ. Calling is not "something." It is the wonderful invitation of God's Son to allow Him by His Spirit to use you as an expression of Him. Finally, anointing is not "something." It is Him moving through your spirit, soul, and body to present Himself to others.

> He who has the Son has life; he who does not have the Son of God does not have life. (1 John 5:12)

> But as many as received Him, to them He gave the right to become children of God, to those who believe in His name. (John 1:12)

Ministry is bringing the Lord Jesus into view. Any ministry that does not do that is not the ministry of the Holy Spirit. Only the Lord Jesus by His Spirit can do the work of God. Any ministry that does not bring Him on the scene will be tested by fire and proved of no value.

CHAPTER 5: CONCLUSION TO PART ONE

- Christianity is not a doctrine to be heard and obeyed.

- Christianity is not a truth to be believed.

- Christianity is not knowledge to be learned by the few enlightened ones.

- Christianity is a Person. It is experiencing and knowing the Lord Jesus.

Paul said even at the end of his life:

7 But what things were gain to me, these I have counted loss for Christ. 8 Yet indeed I also count all things loss for the excellence of the knowledge of Christ Jesus my Lord, for whom I have suffered the loss of all things, and count

them as rubbish, that I may gain Christ 9 and be found in Him, not having my own righteousness, which is from the law, but that which is through faith in Christ, the righteousness which is from God by faith; 10 that I may know Him and the power of His resurrection, and the fellowship of His sufferings, being conformed to His death. (Philippians 3:7-10)

You Cannot Educate Someone into Being a Christian

- Christianity is not a "thing" or a "gift."
- Christianity is knowing Him as dwelling within us.

God gave us only one gift — His Son! Everything else is discovered by exploring and experiencing Him... "For God so loved the world that he gave his one and only Son, that whoever believes in him shall not perish but have eternal life" (John 3:16 NIV).

36 Whoever believes in the Son has eternal life,

but whoever rejects the Son will not see life,

for God's wrath remains on them. (John 3:36)

PART TWO:
HIS UNIVERSALITY

CHAPTER 6: INTRODUCTION TO PART TWO

22 And He put all things under His feet, and
gave Him to be head over all things to the
church [The Church-Ekklesia] 23 which is His
body, the fullness of Him who fills all in all.
(Ephesians 1:22-23)

God has singled out a Person. He has gathered into that Person all the Divine perfections, everything is inseparably bound up with His Son. Firstly, His own nature is exactly imprinted in the nature of Christ.

1 God, who at various times and in various
ways spoke in time past to the fathers by the

prophets, 2 has in these last days spoken to us by His Son, whom He has appointed heir of all things, through whom also He made the worlds; 3 **who being the brightness of His glory and the express image of His person, and upholding all things by the word of His power**, when He had by Himself purged our sins, sat down at the right hand of the Majesty on high (Hebrews 1:1–3 *emphasis added*).

God the Father has put all the fulness of eternity and the universe into that Person. He has bound up all the fulness in Him, and not a fragment can be had apart from Him. That which is to be the very character of the new creation is in Him, and the eternal purpose and predestined end of God is a full presentation of the fulness of Christ throughout the earth and the universe.

CHAPTER 7: THE UNIVERSE WILL SPEAK OF CHRIST

"Every corner of the universe will speak audibly of Jesus Christ" (T.A.S.)!

27 To them God has chosen to make known among the Gentiles the glorious riches of this mystery, which is Christ in you, the hope of glory. (Colossians 1:27 NIV)

1 The heavens declare the glory of God; the skies proclaim the work of his hands.

(Psalm 19:1 NIV)

When the heavens declare the glory of God, it is the glory of Christ that they declare. The firmament shows the handiwork of Christ, the Word made flesh Who dwelt among us and lives at the right hand of God in power and will come again in blazing glory. To be in heaven one day will be to be in the light of God in Christ. To bring down heaven to earth is to walk in His presence.

This is heaven — you walking in the presence of the Lord Jesus. Think of the whole universe like that — a universal expression of His Son in fullness!

This is the end (*telos* - goal) that God has in view. Christ shall fill all things; when I investigate anything in the universe, it will be full of Christ. It was made for Him and in the new creation everything will speak of His presence and show forth some characteristic of His glory.

God has singled out a Person and set Him forth to be seen of all — the man Christ Jesus!

CHAPTER 8: THE UNIVERSALITY OF THE *EKKLESIA*, THE CHURCH

It's impossible to go outside of the A to Z in the realm of language or literature. You are boxed in the totality of language with A to Z. Jesus was the first (*prōtos*) and last (*eschatos*) of God's new creation. Everything in between is in Him!

> 12 And behold, I am coming quickly, and My reward is with Me, to give to every one according to his work. 13 I am the Alpha and the Omega, the Beginning and the End, the First and the Last. (Revelation 22:12–13)

We must never think of anything as outside of Christ. He is salvation, sanctification; He is redemption, justification, wisdom, love, peace, heaven, and He is in us when we are in Him.

> 5 Know you not as *to your own selves* that Jesus Christ is in you! (2 Corinthians 13:5b *emphasis* added)

> 16 Don't you know that you yourselves are God's temple and that God's Spirit dwells in your midst? (1 Corinthians 3:16)

This Person, this Christ — in you! See the possibilities and universal extension of this! What could it mean for the life of the *Ekklesia* to grasp this? The indwelling Spirit of Christ is not something that we have at certain times. It is rather a fact of our existence twenty-four hours a day, seven days per week.

There is no fact more important to our understanding of our own existence than this union. Abiding in the Son and the Son's abiding in us is everything. It is the all in all of our lives on earth, and it is the "beginning and the end" of everything that we do, doing it all "for the glory of God" (1 Corinthians 10:31).

If we are to mature, and if the *Ekklesia* is to mature, it is by being filled with Spirit to the full measure of the stature of Christ (Ephesians 4:13).

CHAPTER 9: GOD WILL TRANSFORM HIS UNIVERSE FROM WITHIN

God will transform the universe not from *without*, but from *within*! How will He transform it? By putting Jesus Christ within the believer by His Holy Spirit. This gracious act will release a two-fold action. First it is the means to being conformed to Him by His indwelling Spirit. He (Jesus) is being formed in the believer. By these two processes, filling, and forming, God will make His new creation.

Listen as the Scriptures rain down this magnificent revelation.

Colossians 1:27 tells us that:

> 27 To them God willed to make known what are the riches of the glory of this mystery among the Gentiles: which is Christ in you, the hope of glory.

In 1 John 5:11–12 (NIV) John says:

> 11 And this is the testimony: God has given us eternal life, and this life is in His Son. 12 Whoever has the Son has life; whoever does not have the Son of God does not have life.

And from Paul in Romans 8:9 (NIV) we are told:

> 9 You, however, are not in the realm of the flesh but are in the realm of the Spirit, if indeed the Spirit of God lives in you. And if anyone does not have the Spirit of Christ, they do not belong to Christ.

Philippians 3:21 (NIV) says:

> [God], by the power that enables him to bring everything under his control, will transform our lowly bodies so that they will be like his glorious body.

Colossians 3:9-11 (NLT) says,

> 9 Don't lie to each other, for you have stripped off your old sinful nature and all its wicked deeds. 10 Put on your new nature, and be renewed as you learn to know your Creator and become like him.11 In this new life, it doesn't matter if you are a Jew or a Gentile, circumcised or uncircumcised, barbaric, uncivilized, slave, or free. Christ is all that matters, and he lives in all of us.

Finally, we read in Ephesians 1:22-23 (NLT):

> 22 God has put all things under the authority of Christ and has made him head over all things for the benefit of the church *(Ekklesia).* 23 And the church is his body; it is made full and complete by Christ, who fills all things everywhere with himself.

Our transformation can only come from within us where the Holy Spirit of Christ Jesus has made a home for a purpose. The transformation of the world can only come through Christ indwelling the *Ekklesia.*

CHAPTER 10: GROWING UP INTO HIM

We must state at this juncture what life in Christ is *not*. It is not a struggle by human effort. It is not trying to practice certain maxims, rules, or a lifestyle. It is not striving to attain a certain measure. It is none of those things, though Christians commonly believe that it is.

What the Christian Life Is

From beginning to end, the Christian life is altogether this: Knowing the Lord Jesus within. This implies three things: response to Him, continual yielding to His working within by His Spirit, and co-operating with Him as He conforms us to His own image.

Here is a formula for spiritual growth. Jesus said it to His disciples this way: *Abide.*

> 1 I am the true vine, and My Father is the vinedresser. 2 Every branch in Me that does not bear fruit He takes away; and every branch that bears fruit He prunes, that it may bear more fruit. 3 You are already clean because of the word (logos) which I have spoken to you. 4 Abide in Me, and I in you. As the branch cannot bear fruit of itself, unless it abides in the vine, neither can you, unless you abide in Me. (John 15:1-4)

Union with Christ is the secret to the Christian life. To respond to Him, we must abide (meno-dwell, live, remain) in Him. To yield continually, we must abide, we must dwell in Him. And to co-operate with Him as He transforms us by conforming us to His image, we must abide.

We are "already clean because of the word" He has spoken to us. This is the Word of love, the Word of regenerating faith by the power of the gospel, the Word of the Cross of Christ. There is only one choice to make after one has put her or his faith in Christ to save, that is the choice *to know Jesus within.*

CHAPTER 11: WE HAVE ALL GROWN SINCE BIRTH

We have all grown since we were born. What does it take to grow? Another way to ask that question is: What does growth *not* require?

Growth does not require sitting down and considering how we can increase our size. We do not know how big we are supposed to grow. Growth in size is an involuntary process. Growth also does not require determination to grow so much per day. It is not like other goals. We are unable to determine the rate of growth.

Lastly, it does not require painful efforts to increase our dimensions. To be sure, that might be the way to artificially grow our physical dimensions. A bodybuilder is an oddity. He becomes that way by forcing unnatural growth.

What does true growth require of you? Nothing! You just grow. But as we grow, we respond naturally to the laws of growth. God has created those laws. God has built us accordingly.

This principle applies in the spiritual realm. We recognize the laws of growth and respond to them so as not to arrest growth. In the physical realm, growth can be stunted by our behaviors. We can get in the way of what comes naturally. In the spiritual realm we can do the same if we do not respond to the laws of growth.

Here is a formula for spiritual growth:

18 All of us, with no covering on our faces,
show the shining-greatness of the Lord as in a
mirror. All the time we are being changed to
look like Him, with more and more of His

shining-greatness. This change is from the Lord Who is the Spirit.

(2 Cor 3:18 NLT)

Ours is simply to abide and behold, to rest in Him. God does the work.

CHAPTER 12: THE HINDRANCE TO GROWTH

The hindrance to growth is the regarding of "things" as apart from the person, Jesus Christ. We think of His benefits as "things" in themselves instead of expressions of Him.

He is not primarily my Savior; He is my *salvation*. He is not primarily my Sanctifier; He is my *sanctification*. He does not anoint me; He is my *anointing*. He does not give me peace; He is my *peace*. He does not bring my joy; He is my *joy*.

A correct appreciation of all that Jesus *is* gets rid of all the strain of spiritual growth. He is the A and the Z (the Alpha and Omega) of our lives and all in between. Growth is the outcome of being focused on Him, not His gifts. Whole movements that have begun by a gazing on the beauty of Christ to the point where He poured out His Spirit and His gifts on the Church, have dried up as the Church shifts her gaze to the gifts themselves. When there is an obsessive focus on the Kingdom of Heaven, then what is ignored, or rather, *Who* is ignored is the Great King Himself. This is an error constantly committed by the Church through the ages.

He is the first; He is all; He is in all. This is the measure of Christ. Everything is bound up with the Lord Jesus Himself.

It's all a matter of knowing the Lord in our hearts. The gospel of God is: We are saved to be conformed to the image of His Son. To come to the fulness of the measure of Christ, "Till we all come to the unity of the faith and of the knowledge of the Son of God, to a perfect man, to the measure of the stature of the fullness of Christ" (Ephesians 4:13).

ABOUT THE AUTHOR

Dr. Ronald E. Cottle has been serving the body of Christ for more than six decades. He has extensive experience in teaching, pastoring, public speaking, education administration and both radio and television.

He has developed more than one hundred advanced courses of Christian development and biblical training and has authored more than one hundred books encompassing ministry, leadership, biblical studies, and church development.

Dr. Cottle's teaching style has been called "scholarship on fire" by those who have attended his lectures. His unique style always contains the compassion of a shepherd, the urgency of a prophet and the wisdom of a statesman.

His thoughts and counsel are straightforward, dynamic, and powerful. His teachings will help today's spiritual leaders and other sincere "thinking Christians" to discover the mystery and the majesty of the Bible.

Dr. Cottle has earned a Bachelor of Arts (A.B.) degree from Florida Southern College, Lakeland, Florida; a Master of Divinity (M.Div.) from Lutheran Theological Seminary, Columbia, South Carolina; and a Doctor of Philosophy (Ph.D.) in Religion from the University of Southern California, Los Angeles. He also earned a Master of Science in Education (M.S.Ed.) and a Doctor of Education (Ed.D.) from U.S.C.

For more information about Dr. Ron Cottle and his numerous books and teachings, go to: www.roncottle.com.

THE COTTLE LIBRARY

Dr. Cottle has worked tirelessly in his home office for the past two decades compiling his five hundred notebooks, fifty plus college courses, fifty plus books, hundreds of sermon outlines, publications, articles, and newsletters. Dr. Cottle and Dr. Thomas Hale are cataloging everything into an online library.

The library contains digital files (PDF and Microsoft Word) available for download, streaming audio files and streaming video files.

Please visit the library at: www.cottlelibrary.com.